THE GOSPEL

AT

COLONUS

ADAPTATION AND ORIGINAL LYRICS BY

LEE BREUER

ADAPTED LYRICS BY BOB TELSON
AND LEE BREUER

MUSIC BY BOB TELSON

THEATRE COMMUNICATIONS GROUP

Book by Lee Breuer, original lyrics by Lee Breuer, adapted lyrics by Bob Telson and Lee Breuer. (Original music, not contained in this edition, by Bob Telson.)

The Gospel at Colonus is published by Theatre Communications Group, Inc., 520 Eighth Avenue, 24th Floor, New York, NY 10018-4156.

Based on an adaptation of Sophocles' *Oedipus at Colonus* in the version by Robert Fitzgerald and incorporating passages from both Sophocles' *Oedipus Rex* and *Antigone* in the versions by Dudley Fitts and Robert Fitzgerald, which are published as *The Oedipus Cycle of Sophocles*, a Harvest/HBJ Book, Harcourt Brace Jovanovich, Inc.

Produced on Broadway, 1988, by Dodger Productions, Liza Lorwin, Louis Busch Hager, Playhouse Square Center and Fifth Avenue Productions; Executive Producers: Michael David, Edward Strong and Sherman Warner.

Early development sponsored by Re.Cher.Chez. Studio, Executive Director: Liza Lorwin, Artistic Directors: Lee Breuer and Ruth Maleczech.

Originally produced by the Brooklyn Academy of Music Next Wave Festival, Harvey Lichtenstein, Executive Producer, Joseph V. Melillo, Producer, in association with Liza Lorwin and Walker Art Center.

On the cover: Morgan Freeman. All photographs by Martha Swope, copyright © 1988.

This publication is made possible in part with public funds from the New York State Council on the Arts, a State Agency.

TCG books are exclusively distributed to the book trade by Consortium Book Sales and Distribution, 1045 Westgate Drive, St. Paul, MN 55114.

Library of Congress Cataloging-in-Publication Data

Breuer, Lee.
The gospel at Colonus / adapted by Lee Breuer ; original lyrics by
Lee Breuer ; adapted lyrics by Lee Breuer and Bob Telson.
Adaptation of: Oedipus at Colonus / Sophocles.
ISBN-10 0-930452-94-1
ISBN-13 978-0-930452-94-0
1. Oedipus (Greek mythology)—Drama. I. Telson, Bob.
II. Sophocles. Oedipus at Colonus. III. Title.
PS3552.R415G67   1989
812'.54—dc19   89-4399
                                            CIP

Design and composition by The Sarabande Press

First Edition, June 1989
Fifth Printing, May 2007

THE
GOSPEL
AT
COLONUS

FOR LIZA

PRODUCER AND SUSTAINER OF

THE GOSPEL AT COLONUS

IN MEMORIAM

JESSE JAMES FARLEY—SOUL STIRRER

1915–1988

ACKNOWLEDGMENTS

Zora Neale Hurston made the connection between Greek tragedy and the sanctified church many years ago. *The Gospel at Colonus,* in fact, could be said to attempt a proof of her hypothesis.

As was the classic Greek performance, the Pentecostal service is a communal catharsis which forges religious, cultural and political bonds. Should not the living experience teach us something of the historical one?

Brooklyn's Institutional Radio Choir says: "Music is our ministry." The living heritage of Africa's oral culture, informing Christianity, *is* the power of the Pentecostal service. "Music" means preaching and responding and moving and testifying as well as the playing of instruments and the singing of songs. Would not the oral culture of the Homeric age have similarly informed the theatre of Sophocles?

The writer wishes to acknowledge his debt to the composer. Bob Telson's score is a great gift. May it long be sung, played and remembered. And both writer and composer wish to acknowledge, with an appreciation akin to awe, the creative contributions of the heirs of oral culture—the singers, actors and musicians of *The Gospel at Colonus*. The writing down of words and music creates only a body. Performance brings to life a soul.

—Lee Breuer

PREFACE

"For the writing in Oedipus, *I conceive something lifting up,
lifting up to great and easy grandeur of cadence. I conceive a
swell; the phrases or sentences or forms gradually letting out and
opening to a great roll and then folding softly back."*

—Robert Fitzgerald, 1939

When my husband wrote the above words in his notebook
in the late 1930s he was contemplating his own translation of the *Oedipus at Colonus,* and could not, of course,
possibly have imagined *The Gospel at Colonus,* which would
not come into being for over forty more years. Yet, as I
read his words now, they have a reverberating significance.
It is interesting enough that when Robert imagined his
translation he imagined it first in musical terms. But it is
even more intriguing that his first imagination of it was
eventually fulfilled, not only in the poetic music of his
own words, but also in the actual music of *The Gospel's*
recreation.

   A great work is great for all time and accommodates it-
self to a changing world. When Robert and Dudley Fitts

began translating Greek plays, they hoped to make those ancient dramas come alive for modern audiences. They wished to conceive translations that were close to the originals, but closeness to them implied more than word-for-word translation—it also implied the need to reimagine the action of a play, and to translate the spirit of the original into the spirit of a different language.

The Gospel at Colonus uses the idea of reimagining in a striking and original way. The play is not meant to be Sophocles' *Oedipus,* but to be a new play, derived from the original, different from it and yet true to its essential spirit. I remember when Robert went—perhaps with a bit of trepidation—to the Brooklyn Academy to see *The Gospel.* But I remember even more clearly his return. He was exhilarated, as many others have been, filled with admiration for authors who had the imagination, energy and enterprise to see the links between two disparate cultures, vastly separated by time, and to realize their vision in dramatic art. He felt, as I do, that *The Gospel at Colonus* fulfilled Ezra Pound's dictum to "Make It New": it builds on the genius of the past to create something wonderful for the present.

—Penelope Fitzgerald

Penelope Fitzgerald teaches English at Yale University and is editor of The Yale Review.

NOTE ON PERFORMANCE

From the very beginning black preaching was different from white preaching. It broke all the rules of form and organization. One of the main characteristics of black preaching is storytelling. The black preacher must be a master storyteller. In the past there was a script that even those who were illiterate knew. The script was made up from the Bible stories, scriptures and songs that had been passed on. The black preacher not only had to know the script. He had to be able to make the story come alive and at the same time stick with the story because the folk he was preaching to knew the story.

In black preaching the preacher has to get outside of himself, or in church language, let the spirit take control. In order for the people to judge the preacher's call to the ministry authentic, at some point in the sermon he has to lose his cool because he isn't supposed to be in charge anyway.

Black preaching is body and soul. Black preaching like black religion is holistic. It engages the whole person. One of the clear things we can say is that the black religious experience is not just a meeting of the minds. It is an encounter with the living God. When we first started serving God, we didn't serve him with our words, we didn't serve him with our ideas, we danced him. We praised him with our whole being.

What implications does this have for drama? Well, in reality, what I do every Sunday is drama, but I am performing for the Lord.

—Earl F. Miller

The Rev. Earl F. Miller performed the role of Pastor Theseus in the Broadway production of Gospel at Colonus. *This note is excerpted from the portion of a 1986 lecture delivered at the Yale School of Drama that was printed in the Guthrie Theater program.*

NOTE ON PRODUCTION

The Gospel at Colonus is an oratorio set in a black
Pentecostal service, in which Greek myth replaces Bible
story. It is sung, acted and preached by the characters of
the "play" — Preacher, Pastor, Evangelist — who take the
roles of the oratorio — Oedipus, Theseus, Antigone. The
preaching addresses the audience directly in rhetorical
styles ranging from the intimate to the musically "tuned"
chant. Choir serves as onstage congregation, and responds
throughout. Organ underscores sermon and scene.

ABOUT THE PLAY

Lee Breuer and Bob Telson developed *The Gospel at Colonus* as a companion piece to their "doo-wop opera" *Sister Suzie Cinema*. In this form it was played on tour in the U.S. and Europe by Ben Halley, Jr. and Fourteen Karat Soul. The greatly expanded version of *Gospel* was first presented as part of the Brooklyn Academy of Music's Next Wave Festival on November 8, 1983. The work was adapted and directed by Breuer, with music composed, arranged and directed by Telson. The production design was by Alison Yerxa, costumes were by Ghretta Hynd', and lighting was by Julie Archer. The cast was as follows:

PREACHER OEDIPUS	*Morgan Freeman*
SINGER OEDIPUS	*Clarence Fountain*
EVANGELIST ANTIGONE	*Isabell Monk*
PASTOR THESEUS	*Carl Lumbly*
SINGER ISMENE	*Jevetta Steele*
DEACON CREON	*Robert Earl Jones*
TESTIFIER POLYNEICES	*Kevin Davis*
CHORAGOS	*Martin Jacox*
BALLADEER	*Sam Butler, Jr.*

CHOIR	*The Institutional Radio Choir*
SOLOISTS	*Willie Rogers*
	J.D. Steele
	Jearlyn Steele-Battle
	Carolyn Johnson-White

In addition to the Choir, musical groups included Clarence Fountain and the Five Blind Boys of Alabama (Clarence Fountain, Rev. Olice Thomas, J.T. Clinkscales, Joseph Watson, Sam Butler, Hardric Seay), J.J. Farley and the Soul Stirrers (J.J. Farley, Martin Jacox, Willie Rogers, Ben Odom, Jackie Banks), J.D. Steele Singers (J.D. Steele, Jevetta Steele, Jearlyn Steele-Battle, Frederick Steele) and The Bob Telson Band (Sam Butler, Leroy Clouden, Luico Hopper, Butch Heyward, Bob Telson, Nelson Bogart, Carl Adams, Curtis Fowlkes, John Hagen). In subsequent engagements Janice Steele replaced Jearlyn Steele-Battle, and James Carter joined the Five Blind Boys of Alabama.

Subsequent engagements took place in Houston, Washington, D.C., Philadelphia, Los Angeles, Atlanta, Minneapolis and Cleveland, and also in France, Spain and Italy. *Gospel's* first Broadway performance was on March 11, 1988 at the Lunt-Fontanne Theatre, where it ran for several months.

Among *Gospel's* many awards are an Obie for Outstanding Musical (1983-84 season). Original cast recordings were issued by Warner Brothers (1984) and Nonesuch Records (1988). *Gospel* was first televised on "Great Performances" in 1985.

CHARACTERS

PREACHER OEDIPUS:
A visiting Preacher who narrates the role of Oedipus and preaches the role of Messenger as a sermon.

SINGER OEDIPUS:
A blind gospel Singer who, with his Quintet, sings portions of the role of Oedipus.

EVANGELIST ANTIGONE:
An Evangelist who presents the role of Antigone and selected choral material.

PASTOR THESEUS:
The Pastor of the church, who takes the role of Theseus.

SINGER ISMENE:
A soloist who, with her Quartet, sings the role of Ismene.

DEACON CREON:
A Deacon of the church who presents the role of Creon.

TESTIFIER POLYNEICES:
A member of the congregation who takes the role of Polyneices.

CHORAGOS QUINTET:
A visiting gospel Quintet whose leader performs the role of Choragos or choral leader and whose soloist takes the part of The Friend.

BALLADEER:
A singer/guitarist with the gospel band who narrates the story of Polyneices.

CHOIR:
A church Choir and its director, which performs the role of the Greek Chorus.

CHILD:
A member of the Choir.

SOLOISTS

PART

I

*A Pentecostal church. Behind its elegant interior is a line of
ancient Greek temple columns. A monolithic pillar stands
down left. One holy place rises out of the ruins of another.*

*Far behind the pulpit, choir stalls rise, fixtured in gold,
upholstered in green. Fans rest on the cushions. A white
staircase descends to a wide landing and from there, by
three steps, to a mosaic floor that sets the space aglow with
color like cathedral windows. Next to the Choir is a gospel
band fronted by a Hammond organ. Center stage is a
grand piano gleaming white but now covered by a tapestry.
On the blue cloth is a vase of gladiolas.*

*The forefront of the stage displays five carved benches
upholstered in red plush—these are for the Deacons. For the
Preacher and the Evangelist, two similarly carved and
upholstered highbacked chairs.*

From floor to flies, serving as a cyclorama, is a great

painting of the Last Judgment, a Judgment more Rousseau than Renaissance, more Africa than Europe, in which all the planets, plants, insects, animals and human beings rise toward us from a panorama so far below as to show the curvature of the earth—part Eden, part Colonus' sacred grove.

A worship service is about to begin. An organist plays and a Choir enters, severally and in pairs, greeting one another. Their robes are a mélange of motifs: church Sunday, African, Greek. Some wear headscarves, other sashes. Many have handkerchiefs tied to their wrists. One carries African finger cymbals, another a tambourine.

The band appears. Between Choir and band members there are warm greetings. A professional gospel Quintet, stylishly uniformed, enters after the Choir. Guests of the church for this special service, the singers create a stir. Then comes the Evangelist in yellow, who takes her place high on the soloists' platform. She is followed by the Pastor in a white suit. Finally, as the house dims and the stage brightens, the Preacher enters with a leather-bound text, which he places on the pulpit and thumbs the leaves thereof. A hush falls over the assembly as he finds his place and reads.

THE WELCOME AND QUOTATIONS

PREACHER:
Think no longer that you are in command here,
But rather think how, when you were,
You served your own destruction.

Welcome, brothers and sisters.
I take as my text this evening the Book of Oedipus.

(He begins to preach)
Oedipus! Damned in his birth, in his marriage damned,
Damned in the blood he shed with his own hand!

Oedipus! So pitifully ensnared in the net of his own
destiny . . .

Net of incest, mingling wives, sisters, mothers,
With fathers, sons, brothers.

You have heard of Jocasta, whose husband was by her
husband,
Whose children were by her child.

How the wretched Oedipus found her body swinging
From the cruel cord she had noosed about her neck.
How a great sob broke from him, heartbreaking to hear,
As he loosed the rope and lowered her to the ground.

I would blot out from my mind what happened next!
For they say this king ripped from her gown the golden
brooches
That were her ornaments, and raised them, and plunged
them down
Straight into his own eyeballs, crying, "No more,
No more shall you look on the misery about me,
The horrors of my own doing! Too long you have known
The faces of those whom I should have never seen,
Too long been blind to those for whom I was searching!
From this hour, go in darkness!"

And as he spoke, he struck at his eyes—
Not once, but many times; and the blood burst
From his ruined sockets like red hail.

Net of blood! His father's blood,

His own blood, shed by his own hand.

In Exodus where it speaks of his death in a place called
Colonus . . . which was sacred . . .
And his redemption there . . .
We direct you to lines 275 through 279,
Wherein he cries out to his daughters:
"I could say much to you, if you could understand me.
But as it is, I have only this prayer for you:
Live where you can. Be as happy as you can—
Happier, please God, than God has made your father."

THE INVOCATION: "LIVE WHERE YOU CAN"

CHOIR:
Don't go . . . away . . .
Father . . . won't you stay . . .

SOLOIST:
Let every man consider his last day
When youthful pleasures have faded away
Can he look at his life without pain?
Let every child remember how to pray
For the lost of the earth to find the way
And the kingdom of Heaven reign

CHOIR *(Rising)*:
Live where you can
Be happy as you can
Happier than God has made your father
Live where you can
Be happy as you can
For he may not be here tomorrow

SOLOIST:

O Father let the singer sing for thee
Let word and song and harmony
Be mightier than the sword
O vision holy vision come to me
Let word and song and harmony
Be a sound like the voice of the Lord

CHOIR:

Live where you can
Be happy as you can
Happier than God has made your father
Live where you can
Be happy as you can
For he may not be here tomorrow

Don't go . . . away . . . O Father . . . won't you stay?

RECAPITULATION FROM *OEDIPUS THE KING*

> *Enter a Singer, aged and blind, who sings portions of the role of Oedipus.*

EVANGELIST *(Over the music)*:
Men of Thebes: look upon Oedipus.

This is the king who solved the famous riddle
And towered up, most powerful of men.
No mortal eyes but looked on him with envy,
Yet in the end ruin swept over him.

Let every man in mankind's frailty
Consider his last day; and let none
Presume on his good fortune until he find
Life, at his death, a memory without pain. Amen.

Music ends.

SINGER OEDIPUS:
Daughter! Sister!

PASTOR *(Organ under):*
Alas for the seed of men.

What measure shall I give these generations
That breathe on the void and are void
And exist and do not exist?

> *The Evangelist leaves her podium. Moving as in a dream,*
> *she descends the white staircase and crosses the stage to the*
> *Singer. As she moves, she takes on the role of Antigone.*

Majestic Oedipus!
O naked brow of wrath and tears,
O change of Oedipus!
I who saw your days call no man blest—
Your great days—like ghosts gone.

Of all men ever known
Most pitiful is this man's story.

All eyes fail before time's eye,
All actions come to justice there.
Though never willed, though far down
The deep past, your bed, your dread sirings,
Are brought to book at last.

Child by Laius doomed to die,
Then doomed to lose that fortunate little death—
Would God you never took breath in this air that
With my wailing lips I take to cry:

For I weep the world's outcast.

I was blind! And now I can tell why;
Asleep! For you had given ease of breath
To Thebes, while the false years went by.

Antigone clasps her father's hands.

SINGER OEDIPUS:
Daughter!

PREACHER:
He speaks, saying:
"Daughter! Daughter of a blind old man . . ."

SINGER OEDIPUS:
Where have we come to . . .

PREACHER:
"Where have we come to now, Antigone?"

SINGER OEDIPUS:
Who will be kind to me?

PREACHER:
Who will be kind to Oedipus this evening?
And give alms . . .

SINGER OEDIPUS:
Who will give alms?

PREACHER:
"Who will give alms to the wanderer?"
Though he ask little and receive still less!

SINGER OEDIPUS:
That's all right.

PREACHER:
It is sufficient.

"Suffering and time," he says, suffering and time,
Vast time, have been his teachers in contentment.
"But now, child . . ."

SINGER OEDIPUS:
Now, child.
If you can find a resting place . . .

PREACHER:
"Child.
If you can find a resting place . . ."

EVANGELIST ANTIGONE:
I see a man not far away.
Father, you must ask what place this is.

> *A soloist with the Choragos Quintet takes the role of
> The Friend.*

SINGER OEDIPUS:
Friend . . .

PREACHER:
"Friend, my daughter's eyes serve for my own.
She tells me we are fortunate enough to meet you."

SINGER OEDIPUS:
Can you tell me, what ground is this?
What God is honored here?

PREACHER:
"What ground is this?
What God is honored here?"

ODE TO COLONUS: "FAIR COLONUS"

THE FRIEND (*Falsetto, without accompaniment*):
Fair Colonus
Land of running horses
Where leaves and berries throng
And wine-dark ivy climbs the bough
The sweet sojourning nightingale
Murmurs all night long

Here with drops of Heaven's dew
At daybreak all the year
The clusters of narcissus bloom
Time-hallowed garlands for the brows
Of those great ladies whom we fear

Fair Colonus
Land of running horses
Where leaves and berries throng
And wine-dark ivy climbs the bough
The sweet sojourning nightingale
Murmurs all night long

SINGER OEDIPUS:
"Fair Colonus . . ."

PREACHER:
"Fair Colonus . . .
It was ordained.
I shall never leave this resting place."

SINGER OEDIPUS:
Daughter, lead me on.

PREACHER:
"Lead me on," he says.

"Lead me on."

Oedipus, led by Antigone, enters the church, the holy place.

SONG: "STOP DO NOT GO ON"

The Choragos Quintet, joined by the Balladeer, rise as one with arms outstretched.

CHORAGOS QUINTET AND BALLADEER:
Stop! Do not go on
This place is holy
Stop! Do not go on
You cannot walk this ground
Stop! Do not go on
Daughters of darkness bar the way
Saying, "Stop!
Do not go on."

They confront Antigone and Oedipus.

Stop! Do not go on
This place is holy
Stop! Do not go on
First you must kneel down and pray
Stop! Do not go on
Till the Gods answer "Yes you may!"
Saying, "Stop!
Do not go on."

Oedipus is now joined by his own Quintet, all old men and blind.

SINGER OEDIPUS WITH QUINTET:
Here I stand a wanderer
On life's journey

At the close of the day
Hungry and tired
Beaten by the rain

Won't you give me shelter
All I need is a resting place
Promised so long ago.

> *The blind men force their way into the church. The two*
> *Quintets face off.*

CHORAGOS QUINTET AND BALLADEER:
Stop! Do not go on
This place is holy
Stop! Do not go on
You cannot walk this ground
Stop! Do not go on
Daughters of darkness bar the way
Saying, "Stop!
Do not go on."

> *Choragos bars the way, lays hands upon the Singer and*
> *confines him to a chair for questioning. The blind members*
> *of his Quintet are seated on benches and represent Deacons.*

CHORAL DIALOGUE: "WHO IS THIS MAN?"

CHORAGOS *(Tunes up with organ)*:
Who is this man?
What is his name?
Where does he come from?

PREACHER:
And when he heard that, he was afraid,
And he turned to his daughter and said:
"God in Heaven, what will become of me now, child?"

EVANGELIST:
And she said:
"Tell them, Father, you cannot hide."

CHORAGOS:
Who is this man?
What is his name?
Where does he come from?
What is his race?
Who was his father?

    The Preacher assumes the role of Oedipus.

PREACHER OEDIPUS:
My father was Laius of the race Labdacidae.
Do not ask my name, my star was unspeakable.

CHORAGOS:
Speak!

PREACHER OEDIPUS:
I am the accursed. I am Oedipus.

EVANGELIST:
And while he suffers there comes a woman
Riding a pony and wearing a wide hat . . . crying . . .

ISMENE COMES TO COLONUS: "HOW SHALL I SEE YOU THROUGH MY TEARS"

    Ismene, a gospel singer, is attended by two men and a
    woman. Together they are the Ismene Quartet.

QUARTET:
Father! Sister!

EVANGELIST ANTIGONE:
She is Ismene.
Princess of Thebes,
Sister and daughter to the accursed,
Sister to me.

ISMENE:
Father, Sister, dearest voices,
I have found you and I don't know how
Father, Sister — I hear your voices
Am I dreaming? Are you here right now?

QUARTET:
How shall I see you through my tears?
How shall I see you through my tears?
How shall I see you through my tears?

ISMENE:
Father, Sister, the Gods have spoken
I bring a promise, a holy vow
A world that casts you down forgives you
And those who blamed you sing your praises now

QUARTET:
Destiny brings you back to me

SINGER OEDIPUS:
Child I'm so glad you're here
It was meant to be, it's a prophecy

ISMENE:
All your suffering and pain
Has not been borne in vain

SINGER OEDIPUS:
I've been waiting for a sign

To ease my troubled mind

NARRATIVE OF ISMENE

> *The Evangelist speaks over the music. The men of Ismene's*
> *Quartet silently enact the struggle of the sons of Oedipus.*

EVANGELIST:
She tells how his sons Polyneices and Eteocles
Began to itch for power; how they fought
Till the younger threw the elder out
And took the crown. How Polyneices went to Argos,
Committed treason for an army; sold out his city
For the promise of his father's throne.
How he marches on Thebes now.

(To Oedipus)
Brother, the traitor, marches on brother, the usurper,
And, trembling at his coming, Thebes calls for you.

PREACHER OEDIPUS:
For me?

EVANGELIST ANTIGONE:
Thebes calls for you to be a shield against your son.

PREACHER OEDIPUS:
Will my soul rest satisfied?
Will Thebes bury me in Theban ground?

EVANGELIST ANTIGONE:
Father! No, your father's blood forbids it.

PREACHER OEDIPUS:
They will never hold me!
Gods! May their fires of ambition never be quenched.
Let the last word be mine on this battle.

Let them that would be kings of Thebes before sons of
   Oedipus—
Let them kill each other!

QUARTET (*Concludes*):
How shall I see you through my tears?

EVANGELIST ANTIGONE:
It will be bitter for them when they stand
Where you are buried and feel your anger there.
But for now, Father, pray to the Gods whose ground
You violated here. Ask their forgiveness.

PREACHER OEDIPUS:
What shall I do?

THE RITE

> *Antigone describes a ritual of prayer. Oedipus is represented*
> *by both the Singer who performs it and the Preacher with*
> *whom she speaks. Acolytes have brought a low table*
> *containing the holy ingredients described. The ceremony,*
> *while pagan, should recall contemporary religious rituals.*

EVANGELIST ANTIGONE:
You must first bring water from the spring that runs
   forever.

PREACHER OEDIPUS:
And when I have the holy water?

ANTIGONE:
Take this bowl. Put chaplets round the rim.

OEDIPUS:
Of myrtle sprigs, or wool?

ANTIGONE:

Take fleece cropped from a young lamb.

OEDIPUS:

How must I perform this rite?

ANTIGONE:

You must face the quarter of the morning light
And pour out your libation.

OEDIPUS:

From this bowl?

ANTIGONE:

In one clear stream. Empty and fill it again
With water and honey, but without wine.

OEDIPUS:

And when this earth receives it?

ANTIGONE:

Cover the place with olive and pray, Father, saying:

"Daughters, spirits, be gentle of heart,
Accept with gentleness the suppliant."

SINGER OEDIPUS:

"Daughters, spirits, be gentle of heart,
Accept with gentleness the suppliant."

> As the Preacher prays he is touched by the spirit. He stands
> supported by his daughters.

DIALOGUE: THE QUESTIONING OF OEDIPUS

CHORAGOS (He whispers):

What evil things have slept since long ago?

The Preacher speaks as if in tongues. The voice, not his own, could be that of Oedipus speaking through him.

PREACHER OEDIPUS:
Do not open my old wound and my shame.

CHORAGOS:
It is told everywhere and never dies.

OEDIPUS:
Thebes married me to evil,
Fate and I were joined there.

CHORAGOS:
It was your mother
With whom the thing was done?

OEDIPUS:
Yes: and these two girls of mine
Were given birth by her who gave birth to me.

CHORAGOS:
Then they are your daughters; they are also . . .

OEDIPUS:
Sisters. Yes . . . their father's sisters.

The Choir gasps. The Choragos chants with the organ.

CHORAGOS:
Ah . . . pity. Pity! You suffered—

OEDIPUS:
Yes . . .

CHORAGOS:
You sinned.

OEDIPUS:
No!

CHORAGOS:
You killed . . .

OEDIPUS:
No!

CHORAGOS:
You killed your father!

OEDIPUS:
God in Heaven!

CHORAGOS:
Killed him!

PREACHER OEDIPUS *(Now speaks in his own voice)*:
"No! I shall not be judged so.
In me, myself, you could not find such evil
As would have made me sin against my own.
Perhaps our ancestors angered God long ago."

He said, "If there were prophecies
Repeated by the oracles
That the father's death would come from his own son,
How could you justly blame it upon me?
On me, who was yet unborn, yet unconceived?
He wished to murder me, I did not know him.
Before the law—before God—I am innocent."

PASTOR:
Antigone pleads with the people of Colonus.

EVANGELIST ANTIGONE:
Reverent men!

Since you will not suffer my father,
Old man that he is,
Take pity on me and let me intercede.

Not with lost eyes, but looking in your eyes
As if I were a child of yours,
I beg mercy for him, a beaten man!

Hear me!

We are thrown upon your mercy as on God's;
Be kinder than you seem!
By all you have and own that is dear to you:
Children, possessions, Gods, I pray you!

Be compassionate!

For you will never see in all the world
A man whom God has led escape his destiny!

PRAYER: "A VOICE FORETOLD"

SINGER OEDIPUS (*With his Quintet, without
      accompaniment*):
*A voice foretold
Where I shall die
Where my soul shall rest
And my body lie
Where pain unending
Ends for me
Where I shall find
Sanctuary*

*A voice foretold
That at my grave
Down my God shall come*

My soul to save
And I shall be
Endowed with grace
And I shall find
My resting place

QUINTET *(Individually)*:
Hear me
Hear me
Hear me

QUINTET BASS:
O hear my prayer
O Lord, won't you hear my prayer

> *The blind Singer approaches the podium unassisted to preach*
> *over the music. Balladeer sings under him.*

SINGER OEDIPUS:
Ladies whose eyes are terrible:
Spirits: upon your sacred ground
I have first bent my knees in this new land;
Therefore be mindful of me and of Apollo,
For when he gave me oracles of evil,
He also spoke of this: a resting place,
After long years in the last country,
Where I should find a home among the powers of justice:
That I might round out there my bitter life.
Conferring benefits on those who received me,
A curse on those who have driven me away.

Portents, he said, would make me sure of this:
Earthquakes, thunder, or God's smiling lightning;
But I am sure of it now, sure that you guided me
And led me here into your hallowed wood.

Grant me then, Goddesses, passage from life at last,
And consummation, as the unearthly voice foretold;
Unless indeed I seem not worth your grace —
Slave as I am to such unending pain
As no man had before.

O hear my prayer,
Sweet children of original Darkness! Hear me,
Pity a poor man's carcass and his ghost,
For Oedipus is not the strength he was.

Therefore, in the name of God, give me shelter!
Give me sanctuary! Though my face
Be dreadful in its look, yet honor me!
For I come as one endowed with grace
By those who are over Nature; and I bring
Advantage to this place.

SINGER OEDIPUS AND BALLADEER *(Concluding with a call
     and response)*:
*Where pain unending
Ends for me
Where I shall find
Sanctuary*

EVANGELIST ANTIGONE:
Father, Theseus has come.

OEDIPUS IS WELCOMED IN COLONUS:
THE PERORATION

> *The Pastor appears atop the white staircase. He assumes the
> role of Theseus.*

PASTOR THESEUS:
In the old time I often heard men tell
Of the bloody extinction of his eyes.
Even if on my way I were not informed,
I'd recognize him. I am sorry for him.
I too was an exile. Therefore
No wanderer shall come to me,
As he has done, and be denied.

He has asked for grace!
And offers no small favor in return.
As I value this, I shall not refuse
This man's desire.

> *An acolyte removes gladiolas and tapestry, revealing the
> white grand piano. Pastor Theseus embraces the blind Singer
> Oedipus, leads him to it and sits him down, whereupon he
> strikes the Jubilee's first chords.*

THE JUBILEE: "NO NEVER"

CHORAGOS AND QUINTET:
We will never
No no never
Drive you away
We will never drive you away
From peace in this land

SINGER OEDIPUS AND HIS QUINTET:
I stood a wanderer
On life's journey
At the close of the day
Hungry and tired
And beaten by the rain

Lord here is my shelter
A sacred resting place
Promised so long ago

CHORAGOS AND QUINTET:
We will never
No no never
Drive you away
We will never drive you away
From peace in this land

> *They are joined by the Choir, who stand and clap. Reprise*
> *with the full company; dancing.*

CREON COMES TO COLONUS

> *Enter an elderly Deacon who assumes the role of Creon.*
> *With him are two ushers who represent Creon's soldiers. He*
> *interrupts the Jubilee. Everyone falls silent.*

DEACON CREON:
I can see my arrival
Has been a cause of fear to you.
Don't be afraid and don't be hostile!
I'm an old man; I don't want hostilities.

PASTOR:
Creon, King of Thebes, comes to Colonus.

DEACON CREON:
I come for this man here.
I'm sent to bring him. I'm the emissary.
It was ordered and it fell to me
Because I am his relative.

(He sits in the Preacher's chair)

Poor Oedipus. Come home.
Your people summon you. Come home.
I grieve for your unhappiness.
I see you ravaged. A stranger everywhere,
Never at rest, leading a beggar's life,
With only a girl to help you.
Does this not shame our people?
In the name of your father's Gods,
Bury this thing now.
Agree to go back to your city.

THE SEIZURE OF THE DAUGHTERS

PREACHER:
And Oedipus answered Creon thus:

Singer Oedipus and his Quintet sing a call and response.

SINGER:
When I was sick with my own life's evil
When I would—

QUINTET:
—gladly have left the earth

SINGER:
You had no mind to—

QUINTET:
—give me what I wanted!

SINGER:
But when at last I had my fill
Of grief and rage, and in my—

QUINTET:
—quiet house

SINGER:
I'd made my peace — that was the time
You chose to —

QUINTET:
— rout me out.

PREACHER (*Over the music*):
He said, "Suppose you beg for something
And no man will grant it or even sympathize.
But later when you are glutted with all your heart's
     desire . . ."

QUINTET:
Heart's desire!

PREACHER:
"When charity's no charity at all
Then he gives it to you."

> *Antigone and Ismene, now represented by the women of the*
> *Ismene Quartet, are seized and forced offstage by the two*
> *ushers who represent Creon's soldiers. They cover the women's*
> *mouths so they cannot cry out.*

SINGER OEDIPUS:
You see this city and all its people
Being kind to me, so you would
Take me away!

QUINTET:
Evil kindness!

SINGER OEDIPUS:
Evil kindness!
That's the kind of kindness you —

QUINTET:
—offer me!

CHOIR:
You'd take him away
But you would not take him home
You'd take him away
To a prison outside the walls

SINGER OEDIPUS:
You'd take me away
To a prison outside the walls

PREACHER OEDIPUS:
You think that way the city will escape my curse.
You think you'll get reprieved from punishment!

SINGER OEDIPUS:
No!
(He laughs)

PREACHER OEDIPUS:
No! You'll not get reprieved! What you'll get is
All my vengeance active in that land forever!
And what my sons will get of my old kingdom
Is just the room they need to die in!

SINGER OEDIPUS:
Just the room they need to die in

CHOIR:
You'd take him away
But you would not take him home
You'd take him away
To a prison outside the walls—you!

DEACON CREON:
Time brings you no wisdom!
While you were ranting
I have seized your daughters.

Exit Creon.

SINGER OEDIPUS *(He whispers)*:
You have my children?
God help me now.

PREACHER *(Over organ)*:
God help him now. For don't you see
That in taking his daughters he has effectively
Taken his eyes and left him helpless,
As if "standing in the wind of death."

Ode 1, strophe 2, line 6.
As if "standing in the late wind of death."

*The blind Singer feels his way after Creon, climbing the
white staircase.*

Oedipus attempts to go after Creon
And he cries out to him . . .

SINGER OEDIPUS:
*Creon! You who have taken them
Who served my naked eyepits as eyes
On you and yours forever
May God, watcher of all the world,
Confer on you such days as I have had
And such age as mine*

CHORAL ODE FROM *ANTIGONE*: "NUMBERLESS ARE THE WORLD'S WONDERS"

The Pastor approaches the pulpit to preach.

PASTOR:
Numberless are the world's wonders, but none
More wonderful than man; the stormgray sea
Yields to his prows, the huge crests bear him high;
Earth, holy and inexhaustible, is graven
With shining furrows where his plows have gone
Year after year, the timeless labor of stallions.

The lightboned birds and beasts that cling to cover,
The lithe fish lighting their reaches of dim water,
All are taken, tamed in the net of his mind;
The lion on the hill, the wild horse windy-maned,
Resign to him; and his blunt yoke has broken
The sultry shoulders of the mountain bull.

Words also, and thought as rapid as air,
He fashions to his good use; statecraft is his,
And his the skill that deflects the arrows of snow,
The spears of winter rain: from every wind
He has made himself secure—from all but one:
In the late wind of death he cannot stand.

PREACHER:
Theseus turns to Oedipus and says:

PASTOR THESEUS:
Stay here and rest assured. I will not draw breath
Until I put your children in your hands.

> *The stage is darkened except for the high platform, where
> the Ismene Quartet enters.*

QUARTET (*With the Choir*):
Numberless are the world's wonders
But none more wonderful than man
The stormgray sea yields to his prows
Huge crests bear him high
Earth, holy and inexhaustible,
Is graven where his plows have gone

Numberless are the world's wonders
But none more wonderful than man
The lightboned birds clinging to cover
Lithe fish darting away
All are taken, tamed in the net of his mind
The wild horses resign to him

Numberless are the world's wonders
But none more wonderful than man
Words and thought rapid as air
He fashions for his use
And his the skill that deflects the arrows of snow
The spears of winter rain

From every wind he has made himself secure
From every wind he has made himself secure
From all but one . . . all but one
In the late wind of death he cannot stand

   Intermission.

PART
II

At the pulpit, the Deacon who takes the role of Creon recapitulates.

DEACON:
You remember that just before the intermission, I, as Creon, kidnapped the daughters of Oedipus, and that Theseus vowed to find the daughters and bring them back. Well, all the while, Oedipus has been waiting. You remember Oedipus can't see, and he sings a song about that—about how he wishes he could see with the eyes of the angels . . . and find his daughters again.

THE LAMENT: "LIFT ME UP"

SINGER OEDIPUS:
I wish the wind would lift me
I wish the wind would lift me

Like a dove
I wish the wind would lift me
So I could look with the eyes of the angels
For the child that I love

I wish the Lord would hide me
I wish the Lord would hide me
In a cloud
I wish the Lord would hide me
I'd fall like a rain of fire
And I'd lie like a shroud

SINGER AND QUINTET:
Lift me up
Lift me up
Like a dove—

> *A member of the congregation, assuming the role of*
> *Polyneices, rises from the audience as if to testify and cries*
> *out, interrupting the music.*

TESTIFIER POLYNEICES:
Father!

PASTOR:
Polyneices, eldest son of Oedipus, comes to Colonus.

> *Polyneices climbs up to the stage.*

PREACHER *(Rising)*:
Fortunate is the man who has never tasted God's
    vengeance:
Where once the anger of Heaven has struck,
That house is shaken forever:
Damnation rises behind each child like a black wave
    cresting.

THE TESTAMENT AND SUPPLICATION: "EVIL"

BALLADEER:
He sees his father—an old man
He's just an outcast in a strange land
He says:

POLYNEICES (*Testifying over the music*):
I have been evil!

BALLADEER:
Evil—everybody's talking about me.

POLYNEICES:
I didn't support my father.

BALLADEER:
Son didn't stand by his father.

POLYNEICES:
In his hour of need.

BALLADEER:
In his hour of need.

> *Testifier and Balladeer interweave in speech and song.*

POLYNEICES (*To Preacher Oedipus*):
Father, shall I weep first for my own misfortunes or for
    yours?
Father, God himself seats mercy by his throne.
So may mercy restrain you now as well.
Wrongs may still be healed.

Speak to me!

> *Music stops. The Preacher does not respond.*

Why are you silent?

The Preacher turns away.

BALLADEER *(Vamps)*:
'Cause you're evil! You're so evil!

> *The Pastor, as Theseus, enters with Singers representing*
> *Ismene and Antigone.*

EVANGELIST ANTIGONE:
Father, I wish some God would give you eyes to see.
Theseus has brought us back to you.

PREACHER OEDIPUS:
My children, where are you? Come quickly to my hands.
They are your brother's—hands that have brought
Your father's once clear eyes to this way of seeing.

POLYNEICES:
Antigone, Ismene, my sisters. Make him reply.
I come on a pilgrimage.

BALLADEER:
He sees his sisters
Running to their father's side
He says, "Talk to him.
Can't you make him reply?"
He says, "Sisters,
Won't you take my part?"
And they say, they say

SINGERS ANTIGONE AND ISMENE:
Brother . . .

EVANGELIST ANTIGONE:
Poor brother, you yourself must touch his heart.

PREACHER OEDIPUS *(Reaching out)*:
Ah my dears, be rooted in your father's arms and rest.

POLYNEICES *(Testifying before Choir, Deacons and
        congregation)*:
I will speak out then! I will tell you why I came.
I am a fugitive, driven from my country
Because as the eldest born I thought fit
To take my seat upon his sovereign throne.
And for this my brother banished me.

Of this I believe the furies that pursue him
Were indeed the cause—so I hear
From clairvoyants whom I afterwards consulted.

(Innocently)
Then why should I come here now?

BALLADEER:
He's so slick.

POLYNEICES *(Turns to Singer Oedipus)*:
Father! These same oracles . . .
They say that those you bless
And only those . . . shall come to power.
My prayers and those of all who fight with me
Must then be made to you. Great captains follow me.

Men like Tydeus—

> *Enter from the top of the stairs three singers who take the
> roles of Captains.*

TYDEUS:
Stand . . . stand by me

POLYNEICES:
—Atolian thrower of spears,
Expert in the ways of eagles.

Capaneus—

CAPANEUS:
Stand . . . stand by me

POLYNEICES:
—son of Oeneus, who swore
He'd raze the town of Thebes with firebrands.

Parthenopaeus—

PARTHENOPAEUS:
Stand . . . stand by me

POLYNEICES:
—who roused himself to war for my sake.

> *The Captains continue singing under Polyneices, who*
> *appeals now to Preacher Oedipus.*

In the name of these brave men and for your own soul's
    sake,
We your children all implore and beg you
To give up your heavy wrath against me!
Listen! I pray you listen and comply.

(He harangues the congregation from the pulpit)
We are beggars, are we not?
Both of us are exiles, he and I.
We live by paying court to other men,
And the same fate follows us.

But as for him, he lords it in our house,
Luxuriates there, and he laughs at both of us.

I go forth to punish him who robbed me of my kingdom.

(To the Preacher)
If you will stand by me in my resolve,
I'll waste no time or trouble whipping him.
And then I will reestablish you in our house,
And settle there myself and throw him out.

(He kneels)
If your will is the same as mine,
It is possible to promise this.
If not, I will die.

THE CURSE

>   The Preacher, as Oedipus, descends to the pulpit.

PREACHER OEDIPUS:
LIAR!

>   The Singer Oedipus curses Polyneices in song.

SINGER:
Once you held the power
And when you did you drove me out
Made me a homeless man
You are no son of mine

>   The Captains' refrain turns to pleading.

CAPTAINS:
O you break my heart
You break my heart
O you break my heart
Don't do it—don't do it

PREACHER *(With tuned responses from the Singer)*:
Weeping is no good now! For we have placed
A curse on you that I now invoke!

You shall never see your native land again.
You'll go down all bloody and your brother too.
Yes, you shall die by your brother's hand.
And you shall kill the man who banished you.
For this I pray and I cry out to the
Hated underworld that it may take you home.

Justice still has a place in the sight of God.
Go! We abominate you! We disown you!

POLYNEICES:
Father!

PREACHER *(With Singer)*:
Wretched son! We cry out to the hated underworld
That it may take you home!

> *Polyneices and his Captains collapse on the white staircase:
> this represents their deaths at the gates of Thebes. The
> Evangelist, as Antigone, weeping, cries out.*

POEM FROM *ANTIGONE*: "LOVE UNCONQUERABLE"

EVANGELIST ANTIGONE:
Love, unconquerable waster of men
Surely you swerve upon ruin here.
You have made bright anger strike between father and
    son.
Even immortals cannot escape you;
And mortal man, in his one day's dusk,
Trembles before your glory.

PREACHING WITH TUNED RESPONSE

The Preacher, speaking as Oedipus, delivers a meditation from the pulpit. Singer Oedipus, Choir and organist respond throughout.

PREACHER OEDIPUS:
Though he has watched a decent age pass by,
A man will sometimes still desire the world.
I swear I see no wisdom in that man.
The endless hours pile up a drift of pain
More unrelieved each day; and as for pleasure,
When he is sunken in excessive age,
You will not see his pleasure anywhere.
The last attendant is the same for all—
Old men and young alike, there being then
No music and no dance. Death is the finish.

Not to be born surpasses all philosophy.
The second best is to have seen the light
And then to go back quickly from whence we came.
The feathery follies of his youth once over,
What trouble is beyond the range of man?
What heavy burden will he not endure?
Jealousy, faction, quarreling, battle—
The bloodiness of war, the grief of war.
And in the end he comes to strengthless age:
Abhorred by all men, unfriended,
Without company in that uttermost twilight
Where he must live with every bitter thing.

This is the truth, my friend,
Not for me only, a blind and ruined man.

I think of some shore in the north

Concussive waves make stream
This way and that in the gales of winter.
It is like that with me sometimes—
(*Chanting*)
The wild wrack breaking over me
From head to foot, and coming on forever.
Now from the plunging down of the sun.
Now from the sunrise quarter.
Now from where the noonday gleams.
Now from the night and the north.

> *The Choir sings behind the Preacher.*

Hear it cascading down the air!
The God-thrown, the gigantic, holy sound!
Terror crawls to the tips of my hair!
My heart shakes! My soul is salvation bound.
And where my body shall repair,
God's lightning opens up the ground.

> *A clap of thunder.*

Bless his name!

> *A bolt of lightning splits the large downstage column and
> sears the white piano. A strange foreboding light, like a
> solar eclipse, turns the cyclorama purple and red.*

EVANGELIST:

Theseus, the lord of Athens, addresses Oedipus, the
accursed of Thebes.

> *The Pastor, as Theseus, enters from above and speaks to the
> Preacher over the rolling thunder.*

THESEUS:
Oedipus! Heaven's height has cracked!

OEDIPUS:
Theseus!

THESEUS:
Your hour has come.

OEDIPUS:
This is God's work! My lord, I longed for you
To come. My soul sinks in the scale.

> *With blind outstretched arms, Oedipus reaches for Theseus,*
> *who descends and takes his hand.*

THESEUS:
I believe you. I have seen you prophesy
Many a thing, none falsely.

OEDIPUS:
I would not die without fulfilling what I promised.
I shall disclose to you what is appointed for you
And your city. A thing that age will never wear away.

For every nation that lives peaceably,
Another will grow hard and push its arrogance,
Put off God and turn to madness. Fear not.
God attends to these things slowly; but he attends.
You know this; you know all that I teach.

ODE: "OH SUNLIGHT"

> *Balladeer and Choragos Quintet sing "Oh Sunlight"*
> *in trialogue with the preaching of Theseus and with*
> *Oedipus's words.*

BALLADEER AND CHORAGOS QUINTET:
O sunlight of no light
Once you were mine
This is the last my flesh will feel of you
For now I go to shade my ending days
In the dark underworld

THE TEACHINGS

Preacher, as blind Oedipus, miraculously leads Theseus toward the high formal entrance where the Singer had first appeared.

OEDIPUS:

Most cherished friend, you alone may see the place I am to die.

The Pastor gestures to the Chorus, who turn away hiding their faces behind their fans. As the pair pass the pulpit, the Pastor pauses there to recall and preach of this moment which Oedipus continues to enact alone.

PASTOR THESEUS:
And he said unto me . . .

OEDIPUS:
You must never tell it to any man.

PASTOR:
"You must never tell it to any man."

OEDIPUS:
For these things are mysteries, not to be explained.

PASTOR:
"For these things are mysteries."

OEDIPUS:

You will understand when you alone will come on it.
Alone, because I cannot reveal it to anyone,
Not even my children, much as I love them.

PASTOR:

And he could not reveal these mysteries even to his
    children.

BALLADEER AND CHORAGOS QUINTET:

O sunlight of no light
Once you were mine
Now in the shadow of the vale I pray
You warmed my flesh above, now bless my soul
In the cold underworld . . .

    Over the music the Pastor concludes his sermon.

PASTOR:

He told me to keep it secret always.
This way God will preserve us from our enemies.
And hold us and our city safe forever.
We must be mindful of his suffering,
His death and his redemption. And this our land
And all our people will be blessed.

    The fogs and flickering lights of the underworld fill the
    entranceway. The Preacher speaks Oedipus's last words.

OEDIPUS:

Remember me. Be mindful of my death.
And be fortunate for all the time to come.

He disappears.

PASTOR:

Remember him. Be mindful of his death.

And be fortunate for all the time to come.

The Choragos Quintet, with Theseus, kneel.

BALLADEER AND CHORAGOS QUINTET:
O sunlight of no light
O sunlight of no light

> *The Balladeer leads the Singer to his place at the*
> *white piano.*

SINGER:
Once you were mine

> *Resting head on hands on top of the piano, he and his*
> *Quintet close their eyes.*

THE DESCENT

> *The Choragos Quintet, led by the soloist, rise and sing*
> *"Eternal Sleep."*

SOLOIST:
Let not our friend go down
In grief and weariness
Let some just God spare him
From any more distress

QUINTET:
O eternal sleep
Child of earth and hell
O eternal sleep
Let him sleep well

SOLOIST:
We pray to you almighty ones
Let his descent be clear

On those dim fields of underground
That all men living fear

QUINTET:
O eternal sleep
Child of earth and hell
O eternal sleep
Let him sleep well

> *Throughout the song, the Singers of the role of Oedipus*
> *descend on their white piano—their bier—into the*
> *underworld. A violet light appears, as from a volcanic*
> *cleft.*

CHORAGOS QUINTET:
Down, down, down he goes
He goes among the ghosts
Down, down, down below—

O eternal sleep
Child of earth and hell
O eternal sleep
Sleep on, sleep on, sleep on

O eternal sleep
Let him sleep well

THE MOURNING

> *A chair is placed before the open grave. The Evangelist, as*
> *Antigone, sits and mourns. Next to her are the Singers of*
> *Antigone and Ismene, who weep and respond.*

EVANGELIST ANTIGONE:
He has gone. It was not war,
Nor the deep sea, that overtook him—

But something invisible and strange
Caught him up . . . or down . . .
Into a place unseen.

Listen, as sisters mourn their brother
And daughters mourn their father.

O Father! My dear . . . now you are shrouded
In eternal darkness. Even in that absence
You shall not lack our love.

CHORAGOS QUINTET (*Under the mourning daughters*):
Down, down, down he goes
Down, down, down below —

PASTOR THESEUS (*Speaks from the high soloists'
     platform*):
He lived his life.

ANTIGONE:
In this land among strangers,
He died where he chose to die.
His eternal bed is well shaded.
And in his death he is not unmourned.

My eyes are blind with tears
From crying for you, Father.
The terror and the loss cannot be quieted.
I know you wished to die in a strange country,
Yet your death was so lonely!
Why could I not be with you?

THESEUS:
Remember that his last hour was free and blessed.

ANTIGONE:
I want to see the resting place in the earth.

THESEUS:
That is not permitted. He has no tomb.

ANTIGONE:
Where shall I go? How shall I live?
O take me there and kill me too.
Great God! What way is left me?

THESEUS:
Mourn no more. Those to whom
The night of earth gives benediction
Should not be mourned. Retribution comes.

ANTIGONE:
Mourn no more. Those to whom
The night of earth gives benediction
Should not mourned. Retribution comes.

SINGERS AND EVANGELIST:
Retribution comes. Retribution comes.

PASTOR THESEUS:
Rejoice, sisters. He has left this world.

DOXOLOGY: THE PAEAN

A woman of the Choir sings "Lift Him Up."

CHOIR SOLOIST:
Well I'm crying hallelujah
Yes I'm crying hallelujah
I was blind, he made me see

(She stands)
Yes I'm crying hallelujah
Lift him up in a blaze of glory
With a choir of voices heavenly

CHOIR (*Joins*):
Lift him high—lift him high—higher
Lift him high—lift him high—higher

Crying hallelujah—crying hallelujah
I was blind and now I see
Crying hallelujah
Lift him up in a blaze of glory
With a choir of voices heavenly

Crying hallelujah—crying hallelujah
Set him free Lord, set him free
Crying hallelujah
Lift him up in a blaze of glory
With a choir of voices heavenly

(They call Oedipus back from the grave)
Lift him up—lift him up
O lift him up—lift him up
O lift him up—lift him up
Lift him high high high high high high high high—higher
Lift him high high high high high high high high—higher

SINGER OEDIPUS AND HIS QUINTET (*From below*):
Lift me up—lift me up

> *The white grand piano ascends. The Singers of Oedipus
> emerge, clapping, from the grave. The Preacher reappears
> in the high entranceway and descends to the pulpit. All
> dance.*

ALL:
Crying hallelujah—crying hallelujah
I was blind! He made me see
Crying hallelujah
Lift him up in a blaze of glory

With a choir of voices heavenly

SERMON

A child of the Choir approaches the Preacher.

CHILD:
By God's mercy, was his death a painless one?

*The Preacher answers the child with the speech of Sophocles'
Messenger.*

PREACHER:
Yes, you may wonder, "Was his death a painless one?"
That is the thing that seems so marvelous.
You know, for you were witnesses, how he
Left this place with no friend leading him,
Acting, himself, as a guide for all of us.

When he came to a steep place in the road,
The embankment there, secured with steps of brass,
He stopped in one of the many branching paths.
Halfway between the place of stone,
With its hollow pear tree, and its marble tomb,
He sat down and undid his filthy garments.
Then he called to his daughters and commanded
That they should bring him water from a fountain
For bathing and libation to the dead.
From there, they saw the hillcrest of Demeter,
Freshener of all things. They ascended it
And soon came back with water for their father.
They helped him properly to bathe and dress.

*The Preacher begins to chant, and the Choir, Pastor and
Deacons to respond.*

When everything was completed to his satisfaction,
And no command of his remained undone,
The earth groaned with thunder from the God below.
And as they heard the sound, the girls shuddered
And dropped to their father's knees, and began wailing,
Beating their breasts and weeping as if heartbroken.
And hearing them cry out so bitterly,
He put his arms around them and said to them:

"Children, this day your father is gone from you.
All that was mine is gone. You shall no longer
Bear the burden of taking care of me.
I know it was hard, my children, and yet one word
Frees us of all the weight and pain of life.
That word is love. Never shall you have more
From any man than you have had from me.
And now you must spend the rest of your life without
　　me."

They clung together and wept, all three.
Then there was silence, and in the silence, suddenly
A voice cried out of such a kind
It made our hair stand in panic and fear.
Again and again the call came from his God:

"Oedipus! Oedipus! Why are you waiting?
You delay too long. You delay too long to go."

This much every one of us heard God say.
And after a little while, as we withdrew,
We turned around—and nowhere saw that man.

　　*With all the stage responding, the Preacher brings the
　　sermon home.*

In what manner Oedipus perished,
No one of mortal men could tell.
It was not lightning, bearing its fire,
That took him off. No hurricane was blowing.
But some attendant from the train of Heaven
Came for him; or else the underworld
Opened in love the unlit door of earth.
For he was taken without lamentation,
Suffering, or pain. Indeed his end
Was wonderful if mortal's ever was.

Now let the weeping cease.
Let no one mourn again.
The love of God will bring you peace.
There is no end.

CLOSING HYMN: "LET THE WEEPING CEASE"

Led by the Choragos soloist, the entire company rises.

SOLOIST:
Now let the weeping cease
Let no one mourn again
The love of God will bring you peace
There is no end

> *Then the Choragos Quintet, and finally the company, sings the hymn.*

BENEDICTION

Raising his arms, the Preacher blesses the congregation.

PREACHER *(Over the music)*:
Now let the weeping cease.

Let no one mourn again.
These things are in the hands of God.

The service is over. Embraces and farewells. All exit. The gospel band plays the hymn.

END OF PLAY

TCG gratefully acknowledges public funds from the National Endowment for the Arts, the New York State Council on the Arts and the New York City Department of Cultural Affairs, in addition to the generous support of the following foundations and corporations: Actors' Equity Foundation; Alcoa Foundation; ARCO Foundation; AT&T Foundation; Center for Arts Criticism; Citicorp/Citibank; Common Wealth Fund; Consolidated Edison Company of New York; Eleanor Naylor Dana Charitable Trust; Dayton Hudson Foundation; Exxon Corporation; Ford Foundation; Japan-United States Friendship Commission; Jerome Foundation; Joe and Emily Lowe Foundation; Andrew W. Mellon Foundation; Mobil Foundation; National Broadcasting Company; New York Community Trust; New York Times Company Foundation; Pew Charitable Trusts; Philip Morris Companies; Rockefeller Foundation; Scherman Foundation; Shell Oil Company Foundation; Shubert Foundation; Lila Wallace-Reader's Digest Fund; Xerox Foundation.